Ghost Music

poems by

Mark D. Dunn

BuschekBooks

Ottawa

Library and Archives Canada Cataloguing in Publication

Dunn, Mark D., 1969-
Ghost music : poems / by Mark D. Dunn.

ISBN 978-1-894543-63-7

I. Title.

PS8607.U555G56 2010 C811'.6 C2010-905057-6

Cover image: Detail from *Eight Hours in Emerg (Memory Series)*,
mixed media with acrylics and India Ink on sixteen 8x10" stretched
canvas panels, overall dimensions: 32x40", 2008, Maria Parrella-Ilaria.

Printed in Winnipeg, Manitoba, by Hignell Book Printing.

BuschekBooks, P.O. Box 74053, 5 Beechwood Avenue
Ottawa, Ontario, Canada K1M 2H9
www.buschekbooks.com

BuschekBooks gratefully acknowledges the support of the Canada
Council for the Arts for its publishing program.

**Canada Council   Conseil des Arts
for the Arts   du Canada**

For Maria

Contents

North of What?

Big Water

To imagine its size
corral a proton in a thimble.
You are that shy particle
at the boundless centre.

To imagine its depth
trawl memory for the first
eyes you saw, opening
your own to the light.

To imagine its taste, magnify
all that has rained
on summer gardens and the storms
that strip lilacs of their scent.

What You Know

i

By the time I realize that we're dancing
the music has passed through and the mud-slapped trucks
in the gravel lot outside begin to show dawn
in mirrors and cracked windshields.

We leave, still dancing in our way, and walk,
a creature with four legs, down Saint Street,
past the martyr's tower near fish trolleys
waiting for the morning catch.

Nothing happened. I remember nothing happening.
It is a hazard of mining unlived memory
that images end without notice, or lead nowhere.
Is this true? Or did you make it up? Someone always asks.

ii

When I look out the window, pedestrians stop being
pedestrian and become tableaux, feeling eyes
on them as I felt eyes on me: the voyeur-self watching
the observed-self pass through the woods.

That unruled forest we called Down Back
where spruce concealed a valley
that ran in a deeper evolution
and ferns grew sinuous without brontosaur gardeners.

Whatever innocence I may claim
I learned in those woods; abandoned there, too:
in slow crucifixion, the sun on summer flesh,
a daisy-chain crown taking no blood.

If I have lied about dancing and dawn in truck windows,
lied about Saint Street fish trolleys, or the
impenetrable green Down Back, it is to be expected.
I know we are dancing, and need no evidence to prove it.

Bawating

i.

Day begins with the river.

Impetuous shock, and morning steams into cloud.
A resurrection of gulls calling in the fish-stout air.
Machines yawning, the American shore at work.
A freighter winks a rusty stern,
needles the southern locks.

A small country onboard leans over
to see where it began, this naming
of land.

Day begins with the old man
walking his dog along cinderblock ruins

through heel-squelched butts beside the river,

in the sand along the river
where tires kicked away from condoms and beer cans:
exclamations pointing to suburban houses.

ii.

Count the beasts in the river:

a primordial swan
fans vapour wings
rises

while the slough-backed snake
older than its legend
enters the day
curls up from the river
to take the old man's gift.

And every morning
the finless beast
and the old man walking his dog
make stories in the hatching day.

Something passes between them,
or so it seems, until light fables it
and the whole rattling day
forgets.

Habit

The mountain I know
changed in the dawn.
I scarcely remember
the brown light,
the gold in the air around it,
the green life from stone.

The mountain I know
invented all this for me.

The Over Child

Most days raging at long hair,
at bad grades, at the lawn
mowed by a loafer.

And then overtaken
by movies, quivering
grief for a yellow dog.

You never knew
which part of the child
to expect.

It was called getting sentimental,
folksy words
for crazy.

Prometheus Borealis

He slept until they found him.
Bone, all bone and old.
Killed by a stone arrow,
the first victim.

10,000 years making the mystery,
then the present day politics
of where the bones belong.

He clawed out of the ground
into the sky near Gros Cap.
Feet pointing west,
he followed
deeper into the lake,
navigating by shadow. Pine shafts
slashed out along water's edge,
the sun beginning to crest:
sundials on the shore.

Wave fingers, the dense lake hand,
drew him against current,
        against better judgement,
deeper, always deeper, past copper islands,
to the feet of Nanaboozhu—even then,
lives ago, sleeping.
And passing, the man brought his bones
—led by his bones—
across the round prairie;
stone hammers and pelt ruins
left for children to find.

There he stopped to invent sorrow.

Mountains, the spine of the great island, shadowed him.
The world ends here, the mountains said.
So he climbed, slid down the other side,
rustling stone.
Less skin on bones when he touched down.
Ocean salt calling the salt in his blood,
he slept for a time in the river mud.

Hikers found him, stashed his skull
in bushes nearby. They returned
with police and professors, cameras and shovels.

He has never been so popular,
the little man from Gros Cap.

Heat Wave, Under a Sculpture by Haydn Davies

Reading Bowering on the grass
near Algoma Blue by H. Davies.
Those shafts, crossed in the air,
crosshairs or fingers ready for elastic bands,
a beam of shade for balance.

A green joke: mystery ticks on my leg.

Seagulls understand that dessert comes after
bread rinds and fruit; they swoop, fearing nothing.

Most crows are silent
now that all has been said.

I-beams splash, frozen in blue. The red
platform too hot for skin.

Peel back the day from mist as the sun rises:
Moiling dawn, the balance of straw in clay,
the secret recipes for brick,
cities beyond the waving air.

Hear the far engines.

It's already too hot for us
and for the others,
who are us as well.

I dream unenviable silence,
the cool silence in winter.
A year's reward, this sleep.

Now the sun is a battery and defines itself
by what it sears from the ground.

The movement of water
to vapour and back is
as far as I can go today.

The Last Thing About Mill Towns

Asserting lines in the round world
I was born into stunning hegemony:
        fields and trees, foxes in summer,
        crows that follow snowshoes through winter,
        birthday cakes.
We were little guys, workers
oppressed in ill-defined ways.

I saved my hate for suburban kids:
their middle management fathers,
mothers who drove cars and read poetry.

Because everyone worked in the mill
  but some were white
  and some were blue.
Everyone measured by the collar.

The rich owned businesses and the rest
gave their bodies to the war, if the war was on.

We went
when we were told,
stayed real quiet,
prayed over nasty meals,
lived kind jokes in hot garrisons,
fought every devil, carried bales around…

I had a friend I hated.
His father was a salesman
who traveled and spoke many languages.

On weekends I visited that family,
played in the wrecked room. The entire basement,
swollen with toys and books. In the evening the family
sat together and talked.

But I could not talk
and my silence made the food go stale.

Inflatable Jesus

The cross went up a century ago.
Dear old ladies and gents took coins
from children to make the cross
gaze neon, godly, from the clay hills over Bawating.

Now they pass the plate again
to build a rubber Jesus for that cross.
Put him up there, head lolling in the breeze.
On Ascension Day, they let him fly
two-stepping across rooftops
on his way to an American discovery.

A Michigan hunter bored with ducks
takes his shot just as the crown crests a pine ridge.
The hunter misses, and inflatable Jesus,
borne up by wind, moves
to Chicago through Midwest corn and wheat,
east to New York for Macy's parade.

Winter Home

We lived in wilderness.

A solitary line through the forest
to meadow, a stream
and the great clay banks beyond.

Trails in a random grid,
a maze through stubby pines.

Watched.

Crow is watching,
answering the snowshoe squeak,
calling wolves perhaps,
though I doubt it.

Wild drama recorded
across the white land
documented until spring
or the next snow fall:

      A fox skirmish
      leaves a feather halo,
      blood pellets.

And, swinging above, crow waits for stillness.

Continue without stopping.

Thaw

Spring, nearly at least,
and the lake edge
is raw from scab ice
and the sand is veined with kelp,
veined with lost lines and lures.

Walking memory around the bay:

Between rock and water is the infinite wash.
Sound returns with the split lake.
The crystal tear, a wave reaching until the ice is gone.
A freighter, locked in since November, moves again,
flexes its bow to shake off sleep.

I lost my hold
here
last fall.

My name in the waves,
in the bird's mouth, the peeper's
tongue, translated
by the zoopoly to sound nothing like my name.

The wind is chatter through pine
and has no sound but for the things it moves.

All voice is sympathy, after all.

And on this lake I hear the mines in Marquette,
the drowned ships with their last great howl.
I hear paddles from birch canoes
and the evolution of rock into dust.

The Stone Collector

In your pocket there is prayer,
the place where
needs were met
and taken partially home.

Wet Foot

Rocks one day
are sand.

Slow,
but you can see
tide grinding

footslidemarbles.

Rattling shore
comes to forever

sooner
            / later.

I move in stone
while dancing.

Photo

Eating warm plums
on a lawn
slick with rain,

the fig tree
barely in the air
can take the weight
of one more arm,

orangutans posing
for a distant shot.

Back home
they ask,
Who is this?
    and
Why is he swinging?

Lake Esnagi

There is something of a small shell in its name,
this lake found by plane and rail.
There is something of the sun on the lake,
the islands owned by moose that chase
boats as dogs chase cars down country lanes.

No choice then but to twist the throttle,
jolt passenger and baggage to the stern.
Even charging from water deeper than it stands,
a moose can fold a wooden boat without missing
a stroke, swim on to the low marsh
and nurse a chipped hoof—without regret.

Waiting for the lodge boy
where the train dropped them,
luggage and fishing rods stacked
and leaning on the dry banks, no one said
blackflies could make an extra skin.

The lodge boy balances the bags,
packs them in—a jacket for each—and
begins slow, the outboard gargling,
the boat low in the water.

In his back pocket, Keats' poems.
I do not want to know that his name is Percy.

Cortez At Algoma

In a black robe, in a mackintosh and bowler,
in a suit tailored by Italians, Cortez stands on Superior.

Ice is new to him—his heels slip.
The stuck bull (his boots) pigeon toe
through snow. He will not tumble—
God does not fall.

This pantheist bluff worked before.
His beard and good timing
brought him to shore, a serpent.

> *Everyone is waiting for something.*
>   *They might as well wait for me.*

Here they wait for Spring. And although he
is sunned brown, flecks of red in his hair,
Cortez is nothing like Spring.

White pine galleons rigged with cattails
took to the lake at Wisconsin.
The fat bow flattened the marsh,
spilt the harvest, but mostly
kept going. North. Dark waves on the great lake.

The ocean inland sighs, knowing what comes next.

Apology

A shard from the old shore drifted with purpose:
find China, find gold, make orphans.

Trace my name to Ire- and Scot- and Engle- lands
but you will not find me there.

My greater parts were lost in passage,
dropped in the ocean, vomited over rails.

I stand here, an orphan of sorts.
The past for me is yesterday,
and the yesterdays of my mother and father.
The yesterdays trapped on the page.
The yesterdays built in stone.

I am not at home, here nor there.

Dropped in this nest, I grew,
believing I belonged.
I learned of the moved-aside,
the squeezed-out and torn-up people,
the languages more lost than my yesterday,
more lost than the family I do not know
back on the old shore.

Here, roads don't stick.
Spring breaks them. The wind eats brick.

We dig, we melt, we shape
and meet ourselves in facsimile.

The grid world, straight as lasers,
bladed like a prow, is palimpsest on true canvas.

Regret

If you believe in sin,
the woods you walk through,
the clay banks above the river,
and the river on flat stone
are lost to you.

If you believe in sin,
suffering is splashback
from rocks thrown in gardens,
and pain is the knife's blade
in the rubber tire,

the baling twine cut
and the bales crumbling
in anonymous fields.

Miraculous Advancements in Barnyard Physics

The Drought Farmer Questions His Guidance Counselor's Advice

He might have given too much
had the crow at dawn not reminded
that saving a little for the next day
is how it's always been done.

He held back.
Held back when seeds withered
to let the real stuff out.
The sun clamped the sprout heads,
drawing matter into a bright vacuum.

He held back when letters came from the bank,
wanting to slug the mailman for saying,
"Can't be good news everyday, you know."
As if he made the news.

The envelope mined valleys between his calluses.
He left blood webs on the mortgager's pen.

This day was given for one more roll at good luck.
Horse-hair charms like Christmas ornaments
strung along fencing, swept curses from the air.
He hoped.

And he held back when the rains did not.
Too much necessity pooling
in serious knots along the furrows.

And again, when rain forgot what it was about
and settled in mist over jungle hills to the south,
letting earth become powder, he held back.

Beanstalks stayed mum about secret destinations.
Cloud bellies, just far enough from earth to be alien,
were the untouched goal, a target for ambition.

Preserves

In the early days
when broad angels
dipped their blades
across barbed fences
he knew the yield
by the look of the grain.

Pestled in his palm,
kernels whine their lineage.

By taste he remembers knowing the earth.

Without him, his mind
grows wild and snakes
along the strands, uncharted.

Only the set plow and the cut of morning
bring him from the deathly cave.

In the Sleep Season, he wanders
the trick paths below sculpting thought.
He dreams order in matted woods and vines,
designs ritual to excuse the harvest slaughter.

In the Sleep Season, he tallies his hunger
against the store:
one grows longer as the other recedes.
It's a cache so fundamental that preserves
are the transubstantiation of verb to noun.

New strains, blurred in the laboratory,
extend the matter, make the seed hollow
until each crop is grown from husk.

Memories of Wendell

With muck oil, the mind
burns in slow revolutions.
He was never the swiftest bird.
But he got by somehow, made
his way through puzzles and
algorithms to become (somewhat)
an expert in barnyard physics.

He tells it in a different way,
and the story is his to tell,
but mostly we remember
angling the sun to make
bars on the brick wall,
and Wendell pretending to skate
over the planks beneath hay.
He plowed tracks and mounds
in the loose floor. My memories
of Wendell divert to the image:
his flat skull against school brick
and the moaning dance he did after impact.
This I see while driving and
wake to see in mornings, or when
my mind wanders. The laughing sobs
he made while rubbing his head,
hopping and bending through the gravel yard.
I thought, "I've hurt him past healing."
Wasn't it by accident? It would be
years before we'd know
if I'd killed him then.

The Suicide

At the high rung
where the ladder
meets gravity
he paused.

As a child he
was praised
for his humour,
the jokes

about everything
that threatened or
made him fearful,
and now

at the long end
in a series
of improbable
jokes he

put his foot in
the noose to swing
above the barn
floor, swing

on the hemp line
with the rafter
singing above
and dust

fingering down
in clouds.
He saw at last
a hatch

in the roof that
never kept out
rain and a latch
unlatched.

He reached, climbing
the rope as he'd
climbed in gym class
one time,

mounted the beam
and stood until
he could just touch
the door.

And pushing through
he let the grey
light in, but with
some change:

there were always
small differences
in the way light
moves in

and out of doors.
It's different
from each angle
and view.

He climbed until
he pulled himself
through the small hatch
and sat.

The hollow fields
below were torn.
The sky, a sea
on sand.

Clover

Even is odd in the field.

He leads the cattle,
their hipbones finning under speckled hide,
to the pond where noses melt in glass,

and he waits on the slope
with a dead oak at his back.

He reads the earth:
the green ink bleeding
from the water below,
browning as it climbs
to peak in drought at his feet.

His father taught him to pick a favorite,
to make one cow a keystone.
And in that way count the ring
beginning with Clover, ending
with Clover. Otherwise,
he'd count the herd all day—
no end to the circle.

By now, they should lead themselves.
March the humped path to water without him.
But then what would he do?
Only there for the slaughter.

He dreams of bringing the idea of cow to market,
of leaving the herd to the fields
and decoding the bell's flat semiotic
that calls him back to ground.

Ghost Water

Prologue

Every wish corrupts
a star, even in falling—
the brief illusion,
the satanic stretch to earth;
a longing to be rooted,
sensual—is luminous until grounded.

Only the mundane core,
the hard manifestation,
a genetic splash in soil
accounts for this desire.

Neighbours

Half of all that is in the world
is love, and the rest is becoming.
You are part of the subliminal wind,
unthought of music in your voice.

I have seen you walking through parks,
your head down, or up, your eyes glassed
and twitching with the river, a veil
over every heart you encounter.

And I have said Hello
and have walked by
without saying Hello.
Let's not war over it.

We are in light.

> On the moon, a million suns in the soil.
> On the sea, a ship turns saltwater fresh.
> And where on earth do people thirst?

O very heart, I am becoming
silence again, and draw deep
into silence again, the moon
over every heart.
Silence again.

Ghost Music

You feel haunted when I'm around.
There is little to say, and I say it.

Two Thoughts on Unity

i.

At the peak of a mountainous high,
the flat earth is more than a theory:
it explains itself, a read page
that lies from night to day,
cold pole to cold pole,
below and around.

At its edge, the film of breath and life,
buildings in cities and trees in the forest,
all sentient and historical movement
waver like the bug screen
against an autumn window.

It is time to visit the lost mirage,
the water-bent air rises
in lines of cartoon stink above our heads.
We are left scratching wondrous lice.
Our blood shared across imagined boundaries.

It is time to divest in time, to let
the dice scatter and disregard the numbers.
It is time to bury the pedants, smoke the clichés
and move on to an unbound measure
that is neither deep nor wide.

ii

It was time that worried my teacher
when she dropped a B in R-A-B-B-I-T
and threw her speller at the class
because we laughed at the cursive
that would replace our stick scrawl.

When the door opened next
it was the principal who entered,
and remained with us while teacher recovered.
No one touched the prone speller,
and its pages bled on the checkered floor
in the margin between our desks.

Tune Me to the River

None of his fish lose an eye.
Not since greed popped one of his own
on a childhood lake.

Since then he's been kind
and lets the fish take the hook.

He'll go months without a catch,
every day at the dock,
irising the tide,
until his spine becomes the river
and the creatures in the river,
notes heard in the body.

Waiting Room

—the inevitable flare and sigh,
        the unrequited always.

This gift is not fully our own,
only borrowed for sensual moments.

What we are comes through skin
and waits for clues about its nature.

I know only what has happened
and often not that much.

In this possible moment,
life opens into undreamed glades
that roll with sleep.

Understand:
        shadow leaves no tip
        but reclines through the door
        undivided.

Quick Mud

Once again the curtains sneer,
like when you were taken:
      the parting night
      and a pinhole
      in the sky that opened
      wider than a star.
      You were swallowed
      and spat out near a highway
      with gibberish on your tongue.
Irreparably something
changed, slid off the pile,
disintegrated on hardwood
at your feet.

This is my Poem on Drugs

Stout clouds badger the sun
into forgetting its place,
into leaving the atmosphere altogether,
even the idea is gone eventually,
400 times farther
than the moon is from earth,
we are moths, once each month,
and for a day or two before
and after climax, we hum
gored songs to its memory.

Mediating moon prepares the eye
for the angelic swath around it,
the sudden breath when the whole orb blinks,

just like Blake but blinded.

The Fate of Bees

It is cool for May.
Crocuses that pried through snow are gone.
Ghosts from the furnace stack
skirt the rooftop and sprout wingless
to the clouds.

She is at the mouth of the attached garage
with five generations around her.
The new baby is old news.

Her brother needs a root canal
but doesn't know what that means.
It can't hurt worse than it hurts right now.
And no one wants to tell him.

He plucks a fat queen from the air as she bobbles by.
It wasn't hard. Nothing left to her but the memory of a hive.
He brags all the same. 'Did you see that,' he says. 'Can you believe
the speed of the man?' Dinner is called and he kicks the bee flat
on the tar driveway before washing his hands.

Reflections

i.

She understands the weather
by the face on the pond
and has been waiting for rain
all summer, bringing the lawn furniture
inside, closing the windows to save
the sills from water stains,
only to drag the wicker chairs
back into the sun and slide the panes
open when the clouds fall
away from the parroted sky.

ii.

Arguing with her lover, she prefers
his anger deflected on the toaster, his eyes
bugging, the tight brow stretched,
wobbling in a funhouse mirror.
It makes him rage all the more that she
won't look at him. His cheeks get red
like element wires, and she smiles
in a way that brings the door to a slam
behind him.

iii.

The taillights of the Buick streak
in the puddles as he drives away.
His headlights click across the gapped birches
and night folds around the absence.
She stands on her porch listening
to the creaks and splashes of a forest
without sun, or a moon echoing its light.

New in Town

At the café he asks for pot
and the manager springs
up from dish-stacking
to ask what the fuck
he's looking for?
But now he wants
coffee, sensing he's not
in Amsterdam, or anywhere
weeds are allowed to grow.

For T.A.

I have forgotten the shape of your hand,
although I feel it in my own
on the taxi ride through dark lanes.

You, the small one, riding the hump
between me and your girlfriend.

I have too much time, it seems,
and find myself a wedge between lovers,
a bland distraction.

It is my third week of drifting,
asleep in knots on the floor.

In the morning, you make oatmeal at the stove,
the night shirt hanging low from your back,
the world above your thighs uncovered.

Now and then a spray of down.

My thumb traces the scar along your index finger
where the farm dog nipped you back on PEI.
I smooth the cuticles you've bitten raw:
you could lose everything with this ride.

Later you tell me how she defines your love,
like a jealous man, she guards it,
and the thought of betrayal holds you back.

I have barely moved toward you
and you get closer each day.

We drift from there.
I get a job, a place in the mountains.
You leave your girl for another.

The last time I saw you—standing for the bus after trial,
a block away—you cupped your lips with those hands,
shouted, "I love you" with all the judges watching.

That Famous Wish Deciphered as Lightning

It could rain all night
with two cats nearby
great shadows making distinct havens
from the bones underfoot,
and I still would not know
the name silence gave darkness
before their first kiss

Number One Waltz

That sharp
        —DIP—
                  finger
  can follow
           each
              numbered   —TURN—
           step,
      i
     am not
             ... 1, 2, 3 ... 1, 2, 3 ...
    let
      -ting go
           until
         we've crossed
             this
                goddamned ballroom.

Ukrainian Drinking Song

                    joy
                   ful
               love
                   ly
               good
                    w
                 a
             t
         e
          r
         str
             o
                 n
             g
         w
             a
                 t
               er
             turn
                    the
                        whee
                            l
             , make   it
                        e lec tric

58

The Office Knell

It's that morning when the world ends.
Everyone brings unpublished novels to work.

This is why
I was distracted
when we spoke at the water
cooler. This is how
I spent my summer vacation.

Novels no one has time
left to read.

But we pass them around and pretend
to kiss each word,
make up good things to write on yellow
sticky paper, hoping
we get something right, or close.
Notes that say *Good job,*
I like what you've done here.
You have touched me,
    and then,
        Goodbye.

That Ritual With Fire

Smokers in a shooting gallery lineup
march in snow banks to keep the cold out
waving red ends.

They draw in the air
as years ago they wrote
with sparklers
against a moonless sky on summer nights.

A Dream, I Guess

I will never know your name.
Victoria. 1995. Nor will I
describe the house where you lived,
or the stripped room I slept in
after drinking at the windowless bar.

Awake on my back,
you standing above.
A darker form
in the dark around you.

Housebound

I step out of you
and apologize for taking
space from your day.

You step into
commitments involving car keys
and locked doors,
meetings late at night
and migraines that repel touch.

My dinners end with solitary bows
to the television.

I begin to see myself
in the cigarette faces of talk show guests.

And I'm not laughing anymore either
at the deadbeats who screw secretaries
and the secretaries who screw deadbeat
bosses for Christmas bonuses,
the mousy wife or husbanded sweetheart
at home, unsuspecting.

I have done this already:

Chased headlights across window blinds.

There are bits of you
around the house
I sweep into piles.

My daily chore is gathering
the memory of who you are.

The Next Revolution
  for G S Heron

The revolution will be compromised, or passed by—
  mistaken for rags
  and used to mop dust
  so the boss can sit down.
The revolution will be compromised
  over lattes in the backroom
  with the TV muted in the corner.
  And maps on the table
  marked with blue and white lines
  through flat ranges that make jigsaw nations
  from boundless earth.
The revolution will be compromised
  in silk stockings, leather
  heels on the groin
  the safe word slurred,
  muddled by translation, electric clips
  and the fierce sodomy of market shares.
The revolution will be compromised.
The revolution will be compromised.
The revolution is dressed like Goldilocks.
  Paste-on freckles peel in the heat. Walls
  drip in desperate basements. The revolution
  has confessed to poisoning the well.
  It cries in razor sobs, will say what's required,
  sign the contract, endorse any product.
The revolution has a bit in its mouth,
  takes it without complaint.
The revolution has cancelled its subscriptions,
  turned the thermostat past 30
  and left town.

Imagist Howl

I discovered love in a nazi bar
where the unimaginable worst
is implied, and every possibility
an insult to someone.

Ordering a double espresso,
I recant to the long table
in shadow, the one with parts
scattered in a whole.

The gears of clocks, from artificial limbs
are coasters for the bleached cup that frames
teak coffee against the table's waving grain.

Ignoring the howls from behind the wall
we talk as if no one would want
to hear us talking, as if our words are bare

space where the lines have split open.

Copernicus Measures the Dawn, 1513

Candles are the best way for the page to hurdle its shadow.
Sunlight exposes the blank world between words
and oil light sticks to the eye, sheds grease skin on walls.

A moth brought in to attack the wick, or the pert wind
gasping its dictation, might shake the flame
but the wax finger coils down in time to the climbing dawn.

In the space made by tallow, the page is primed for computation:
the spastic run to predict the bend of the world
that leaves ink tracks from the field to the well.

A Love Supreme

To describe Coltrane's reed squeal
we refer to animals in nature
as depicted in storybook recordings:
elephant, walrus, a lion under fire.

We look to the machine world:
to trains, factories, to scrap yards.

And in locked-up places,
the determined hinge tearing—

but find only
more Coltrane.

Toronto (mid 90s)

In T.O.
they got jobsjobsjobs

wanted signs in windows
a saint on every corner

in T.O.

The kid in the bag,
not sleeping,

jostling for coin,
could be happening
in the country, in a smaller place
warmer than here with
more trees from the ground
less honk and wheeze in the air.
        But he's not there, he's here
and he's collecting money
for a political coup.

And I walk by
as every body
walks by,
throwing change
or not,
        unchanging.

Nobody laughs anymore.

He is still, moving through cages

Once confined, he counted the days in sleep
and read the seasons by the way his visitors dressed.

I knew everything about him,
except his name—he would not tell—
and he seemed fine to both of us.
He did not mind, never a complaint

about those bars and the changing fashions.

   Yesterday, it seemed, you wore a toque and scarf.
   Today you're in cap and shorts. Is it summer?

My visits confused him
and I thought to stop coming by
but never found a pleasanter way
to spend an afternoon.

Released, he sputtered at the heels
in the doorway, kicked up dust
and slouched to the cab
and the minute hotel across town.
Red lights dancing in windows.
Red lights shaped like legs, like boobs,
butts, hanging from the night outside his window.

He walked from cage to cage
with the doors clapping behind him.

E—

A seed of itself, that movie destroyed
solitude for a catholic generation.
Fear that one could lose
control, it is mind that attacks in the still dark
More than phantoms: spectral cats yowl in hallways
Neighbours who've never spoken open doors to check it out.

Some lost cat walked in
when I carried groceries from the car.
Only this and nothing more.

If I had a television
Bugs Bunny would be on,
leisurely, about to spring.

A Poem On Returning to a Job I Left for Good

It's not that the bridge has been repaired
or replaced:

the scorched towers, crossed and leaning
like knitting needles after the detonation,
have dropped all weight and stand as memories
in the places we have lived;

the suspension cables are twisted beneath rock dust,
the spring gone from them. Yet it's easy to go back
with the riverbed dry, the water corked upstream.

And everything is just where I left it.
Waking with the previous day unfinished,
its pieces on the table scattered like a fugue.
All that I ever ran from expects completion.

Next time, I take the river with me when I go.

There Have Been Sightings

A cell
white block
boxed in maze.
I live these days
with this room around me.
Silent. Voices under doors:
TV voices and the flipping mood
change. Turning and turning
through the digital mire. Headboards thump
in love's pinched rhythm.
Lunch break. An office romance
behind DO NOT DISTURB signs.
Fresh sheets every hour.
A pillow beneath the mint. Nightly,
weekly, ½ hourly rates available.

Pseudonymous ledger crawling with Smith
and Jones. The desk clerk has seen,
heard more than he remembers
and knows by the way you hold the key
the sort of mess you'll leave behind.

I have been here too long,
it's said. A ghost above ceiling tiles,
I help with dreams and rattle
hallways when aroused.

My fingerprints everywhere,
the main attraction in this hotel
is the silence before manifestation.

Aesthetic Cling

Beauty is blue from garden.

You, above sky, chanting sea petals to diamond.
Whims collide, snake washing sand and foam,
pull out from skin, out of memory
   a word,
            different from all words,
spoken once a life
and usually to the wind
when ears are far and cloaked.
Spoken, or unspeakable,
written in ways the eye cannot decipher,
leaving its sound in soul.

This is the world for which I pray.

        The primordial drip.
         That long first step.
          The pigeon heat in summer.
         Letting rage guide me
        (I am blind to all but rage).

And beauty again presents a beastly face,
slobbers elixir on cavernous wounds.

This is how the world begins:
        one quick seed
        and monumental conspiracy
        tugged into earth
by watery hands.

The Street You Live on is Lonely

There is something in the wine
beyond the memory of grapes.
The event responds to, or does not consider,
its surroundings, happens or does not happen,
depending on the previous frame.

I have seen enough funny hats with nothing underneath;
empty heads crowned in remarkable structures,
with mouths answering for imagined reputations.

It happens all the time that I catch myself
in the mirror as I walk away.
Although I wink at the glass,
I never wink back, and it hurts.

There have been times when I am lucid
at the thought of going.
I am never separate for long
from the parts of myself that remember
the unbroken edge. I am never apart
for long from the desire to swim
under the ice, with the fish gilling
the mute shadows below.

In the end, knowing
what to throw away
before decay decides is balance.
                    I am never long
away from the dock.
The lake does not hold me
without ice to widen the shore;
each side opening to the possible crater that faith makes.

I am not gone for long days, only the tick of the sun
around our backs, across shoulders, and up again
to claim the conversation.

Apology 2

She wants me to believe only the rich make poems,
and scream with her at the ivory men who never gave
the chance to have the things she hates.

I haul out sleepy examples, the dusty giants
from fishing towns and loyalist towns,
prairie towns and gutter alleys.
The ones with earthy half moons under their nails,
the knots on their spines fused and aching.

She answers that each gave up privilege
to hit the road and rails, or to live
on scraps in shacks near the crazy edge
because brief inheritance was too much to satisfy.

Without a conviction seeded in wealth
only a fool would play with words
and expect to be paid.

Put down your pen, she said,
You are pretending.

I tried to believe and would have,
but a sound that will not be named
called, kept calling,
in a language unknown to me.

The Gong of Mew

THE GONG of MEW

i. Invocation

Sing, O Dudes, of the madness of Mew
who came down—a shot from dark Heaven.
The thunders streaming behind,
Mew cursed voice into song
and sang while the soul was dancing.

Overhead, more than clouds,
the twined expectation of clouds:
soft or black, full or flat with rain.

By the time Mew knows the answer,
the simple rains have washed
most certainly the mystery away.
We stand, our feet
bleeding into earth,
and wait for sorrow.

ii. Cosmology

I have seen Mew in clouds,
circling, a halo of sorts
calling the orbits that wobble
the axis of a spine:
inconsequential, never certain
that last will be last.
Before we can blink, Mew shouts
a world into breathing, screams
autochthonous terror into night,
broiling the plain grass,
sending geese on early migration.

iii.

Mew knows the distance between satyrs,
paces the length between their posts.
Mew counts the time through space
from hoof to hoof.

Mew knows the distance between stars.

iv.

Listening to Vivaldi's righteous calm
I saw a goat-boy with Mew.
He looked across the slumped hills
outside a village long gone
and whistled the strings under a cast of wind
and reed, wind through reeds and branches,
while veiled dancers spun in wisped haloes
like May clowns, the crowd unaware—
spent faces watching the horizon
for a change in light.

The seeds are ready for earth.
Is the earth ready for the seed?

Mew waits with the planters,
their long sticks, bladed with shale
or bound to antlers, propped against
the last oak while they sleep waiting
for the sun to wake them.

If Mew seems old, immeasurable,
it is a trick of the day. We see
our time clearly over blinders,
invested in the hard illusion of now.

Mew sees through now as through a distant fog.

v.

The best illusions siphon the eternal.
Let all that stays and remains slip
away and leave the spine
to sputter and construct
this pleasure, that distraction.

There was a boy who met the sun
everyday until time, time brought
a man out from the den to greet morning.
Still, the boy inside blinked at wondrous dawn.
Still the child watched for satyrs in the prancing horizon.

But all around him Mew was laughing
at the parts forgotten, the lot tossed in,
the circumstantial belief until blood
can no longer deny the furious moment.
In that moment, the man counting his tasks
for the day, the reason for watching sun forgotten,
he heard his heart as a clock
ticking trochaic
and each breath a grain rolling downhill, away.

Mew laughed at the hubris of mortality.

Are you so important that you might not live forever?
So rare a thing that you will not be seen again?

When Mew shone gold from the head stage,
eyes and lights at the foot gasping up,
the homunculus slid into the empty seat
and whispered its frailty,
the falseness of any assumed accomplishment—
although Mew never assumed a thing.
Mew had been dancing for centuries,
dancing and letting gold shine from the stage of its head.

vi.

Then, quite suddenly, to life.

The muse cursed his song,
who could understand?

By the clock chop cry overshadowed—
the chuff and weave hurls spondee
at winnowing shade.

Mew has not come here to count,
or to despair over the length of a line.

We find answers where love cannot follow
in the limits of duty and commitment
even the servant's bell drops silent.

Mew is here but is not speaking;
no apology. Hardly a word between us.

On foot for days, Mew looks for a trail.
I do not follow.

There is wind underground:
broadcasts from pneumatic worms
all the people in bellies,
Jonah and the Millennium Falcon,
howl from the buried tracks.

From a dream haze, a forest.
Red berries, the low trail around shrubs
toward a lake propped between gaps in trees,
a blue pane for the distant eye.

The ghost of Mew everywhere I go.

Acknowledgements

Many people contributed to this project, directly, and by being around
as it happened. Mostly, I thank Maria Parrella-Ilaria, for every day;
Cliff Alloy, for years of friendship; Lindsay Pugh, for music, laughs,
and friendship; Karen Smythe and Greg Betts, for friendship and keen
reading; Jesus Hardwell, for fearless insight; Karl Jirgens, for guidance;
Sarah Pinder, for energy and kindness; Mark & Louisa; Colleen Brady
and Terry Hill, for chats and meals; Allan Garshowitz, for not killing
me over chess; Ed Butler, for encouragement when it was needed
most; Jim Zukowski, for being a bud and for insight into the work; Joel
Merzetti, for music, friendship, and peanut butter sandwiches; Gail
Giuliani and Dave Euler, for walks and guidance; Rolland Nadjiwon,
for encouragement; Jeanette, Steve, and Evan, for their kindness;
Arcadia Coffee House, where some of these poems were written; The
Sault Public Library, for keeping a book or two on its shelves; the Art
Gallery of Algoma, for moving forward; students at the colleges and
universities where I've taught; supporters of Read More Books; John
Buschek and all at BuschekBooks; too many musicians and venues
to name; and my family, Evelyn, Charles, Kim, Gerry, Darby, Patti,
John, Laurrene, and all the kids (no longer kids), as well as Tony, Anna,
Shirley, and Gerald. Thank you.

This collection and the poems in it were helped into being by grants
from the Ontario Arts Council. I am grateful to the OAC and the many
publishers and editors who have supported my work over the years.

Some of the poems in this collection have been published in slightly
different forms:

"The Next Revolution." in *Rogue Stimulus: The Stephen Harper
Holiday Anthology for a Prorogued Parliament* (Mansfield Press,
2010); "Apology," *Queen's Quarterly*; "The Farmer Doubts His
Guidance Counsellor's Advice," *The Literary Review of Canada*;
"Cortez at Algoma," "Prometheus Borealis," and "Number One Waltz,"
Rampike; "The Office Knell," *The Dalhousie Review*; "A Dream, I
Guess," *QWERTY*; "Quick Mud," *Jones Avenue*.